Speak in a Week™ French Week Three

by Donald S. Rivera
Illustrations by Julie Bradbury

Published & distributed by

Penton Overseas, Inc.
Carlsbad, CA

Speak in a Week™
French:
Week Three

Published and distributed by Penton Overseas, Inc., 1958 Kellogg Avenue, Carlsbad, CA 92008.

www.pentonoverseas.com

Contact publisher by phone at (800) 748-5804 or via email, info@pentonoverseas.com.

First printing 2005
ISBN 1-59125-427-2

Contents:

How to Use Speak in a Week:

Start with Lesson Seventeen which picks up where Lesson Sixteen of Week Two left off. Continue to follow the lessons in order so you learn everything well. Master each lesson before you go to the next one.

Each lesson begins with an outline of what you'll be learning, followed by ten illustrated examples, first in French, then in English. For every lesson, there's a track on the audio CD to help you with French pronunciation.

On the illustrated pages, you'll also find extra grammar tips, helpful hints, and interesting facts about French-speaking cultures. Following the eight lessons, you'll find a reference section with basic info, more words, and extra grammar.

When you've finished the lessons, go to the audio CD and listen to the last five tracks: The Mastery Exercises. You'll play with the French you now know, so that you'll be able to make new sentences from what you've learned.

You'll be speaking French!

Lesson 17

In this lesson you will learn...

- The different forms of the verb *to be*.

- When to use *it is* or *they are*.

  Use the chart on the following page
  as a guide to the verb **être.**

The verb **être** is one of the most frequently used French verbs. You should memorize its irregular conjugation as soon as possible. Note that a liaison occurs with **"vous êtes."**

je suis	I am	nous sommes	we are
tu es	you are	vous êtes	you are
il/elle/on* est	he/she is	il/elle/on sont	they are

*"on" (one) is frequently used in French. It is the impersonal subject equivalent to the English use of *you, you all* or *they* when refering to things in general.

Note: Verbs not following this pattern are irregular verbs. See **Lesson 27**.

Je suis...

Jacques.

français.

If Sophie were talking, she would say: Je suis française.

I am...

Jacques.

French.

The verb être is used in many idiomatic expressions.
To see other ways être is used, check out
Glossary Page 237.

4

Je suis...

infirmière.

ménagère.

French subject pronouns must be included and are never dropped.

I am...

a nurse.

a housewife.

The indefinite article un/une is not used when discussing someone's job unless the occupation is modified by an adjective. For example, Je suis une bonne infirmière.

6

Tu n'es pas...

fort.

faible.

Adjectives ending in -e (silent (mute) e) stay the same for both masculine and feminine nouns in the singular form. (Michel est faible./Sophie est faible.)

You are not... (informal)

strong.

weak.

Strong and weak describe the subject you and agree with the subject gender and number.

Il est...

 maigre.

 gros.

If a man or woman is very skinny, you can call him or her mince. Adjectives ending in -e have only one singular form.

He is...

thin.

fat.

If someone is a little fat, they are un peu gros. But if they are very, very fat, they are très gros.

Nous sommes...

médecins.

touristes.

Make sure you keep the subject pronoun nous and all subject pronouns when conjugating the verb être.

We are...

doctors.

tourists.

Another way to say doctor is docteur, especially if greeting him directly Docteur Dupont. Note that a female doctor is la femme médecin.

12

Vous êtes...

travailleurs.

paresseux.

Tu is the singular you and takes *es*. *Vous* is the plural you, as in "you guys" or "you all" and takes *êtes*.

13

You are... (plural)

hardworking.

lazy.

Industrieux also means hardworking. Use the -eux ending for masculine and mixed plural; use -euse for the feminine form.

14

Ils sont...

acteurs.

musiciens.

Don't forget, plural nouns require plural adjectives.

They are...

actors.

musicians.

Note that in mixed company (men and women subjects), the masculine plural personal pronoun Ils must be used.

C'est...

André.

Ce can be used with the conjugated form of the verb être (ce + est = c'est) to mean he is, she is or it is. Ce has no number or gender.

It is…

André.

The plural form of *c'est* is *ce sont*, meaning they are.

C'est...

une fille
dynamique.

C'est is used instead of il est or elle est before the
singular indefinite articles un and une.

a dynamic girl.

C'est and ce sont are used for identifying people by their proper names, as in C'est André and for identifying people who are described by adjectives, as in C'est une fille dynamique.

Ce sont...

mes lunettes
favorites.

In this phrase ce sont is used because lunettes is plural.
C'est and ce sont are also used to identify objects and
objects described by adjectives.

21

These are...

my favorite glasses.

One final instance of when to use *c'est* (it is) is when you are referring to something which has already been mentioned. Once you have already stated *Cette cassette est ma favorite*, you can then say, *C'est ma cassette favorite.*

In this lesson you will learn...

- To express the concept of *there is* and *there are:* **il y a**.

- To express the concept of *Is there?* and *Are there?*: **Y a-t-il?**

Use the chart on the following page as a guide to forming the past participle of regular verbs.

In this lesson you will learn to make general statements using the verb avoir (to have). To express the phrases there is/there are, *avoir* takes a special form: **Il y a.**

Whether you use the phrase to express there is (singular) or there are (plural), it remains the same.

Phrase	Meaning
Il y a...	There is.../there are...
Y a-t-il?	Is there?/Are there?
Il n'y a pas.	There is not./There are not.
N'y a-t-il pas?	Isn't there?/Aren't there?

une tache sur
mon blouson.

Remember: Il y a does not change
if the noun is singular or plural.

There is...

a spot on my blouse.

Do you need your clothes washed? Look for une *blanchisserie* (a laundry) or une *teinturerie* (a dry-cleaner).

Y a-t-il...

un supermarché
près d'ici?

To use il y a as a question, use inversion: with the subject
il following the verb a and add the t to help
pronounce the two vowels separately.

Is there...

a supermarket close to here?

If you are in France looking for fresh produce, meat or fish, be sure to go to the local market. It's a great place to practice your French!

Y a-t-il...

des volontaires?

Use Il n'y a pas de to express there isn't or there aren't:
Il n'y a pas de volontaires. (There aren't any volunteers.)

Are there...

(any)
volunteers?

Just as with il y a, the expression y a-t-il can be followed by either a singular or a plural noun.

Il y a...

vingt étudiants dans la classe.

Use **Il y avait** to state there used to be: **Il y avait dix-neuf étudiants.** (There used to be nineteen students.)

There are...

twenty students in the class.

What else is there in la classe? Check out
Glossary Page 214 for a list of things you might find.

Il n'y a pas...

beaucoup de circulation le matin.

Use Il y avait to state there was or there were:
Il y avait beaucoup de circulation.
(There was a lot of traffic.)

There isn't...

a lot of traffic in the morning.

Other adverbs of quantity you can use to describe how much traffic: peu (little), moins (less), or plus (more).

Il n'y a pas...

beaucoup de fleurs dans le jardin.

Il y aura is used to state there will be: Il y aura plus de fleurs en juin. (There will be more flowers in June.)

There aren't...

a lot of
flowers in
the garden.

Study tip: Find a peaceful place to study
and set a regular time to go there.

Y a-t-il...

un médecin dans l'hôtel?

While booking a room in a hotel, you might ask, Est-ce qu'il y a de la climatisation (air conditioning)?

Is there...

a doctor in the hotel?

It's not that serious! You only need an adhesive bandage (un pansement). Look for one in the Pharmacy on Glossary Pages 200-201.

Il y a...

une fête ce soir.

Mastery Exercise: Combien de personnes y a-t-il?

There is...

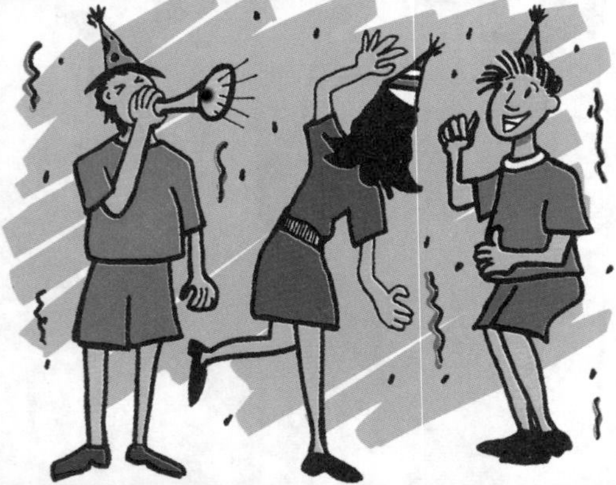

a party this evening.

Mastery Exercise: How many people are there?

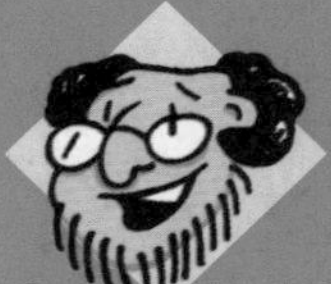

Il y a...

une mouche dans ma soupe!

Mastery Exercise: Il y a trop de sel dans la soupe.

There is...

a fly in my soup!

Mastery Exercise: There is too much salt in the soup.

Y a-t-il...

une place
pour
s'asseoir?

S'asseoir is a reflexive verb. You'll learn more about reflexive verbs and how they're used when you get to Lesson 29.

Is there...

a place to sit?

To be polite, you might ask
Est-ce que je peux m'asseoir ici? (May I sit here?)

In this lesson you will learn...

- To use the verb *to do/to make.*

- Some idiomatic expressions using the verb *faire.*

Use the chart on the following page as a guide to forming the verb *faire.*

The verb *to do/to make: faire*

je fais	I do	tu fais	you do
nous faisons	we do	vous faite	you (plural) do
je ne fais pas	I don't do	tu ne fais pas	you don't do
nous ne faisons pas	we don't do	vous ne faites pas	you (plural) don't do

il/elle/on fait	he/she/one does
ils/elles font	they do
il/elle/on ne fait pas	he/she/one doesn't do
ils/elles/ne font pas	they don't do

The verb **faire** (to do/to make) is often used when speaking of household chores or playing sports. It is used in many idiomatic expressions, including expressing the temperature and weather conditions. To review the many important idiomatic uses of the verb **faire,** see **Glossary Pages 236-237.**

Je fais...

la vaisselle.

The verb faire is often used in reference to household chores.

I am doing...

the dishes.

Il fait froid (It's cold). Il fait chaud (It's hot).
One idiomatic use of the verb faire
is to convey weather conditions.

48

Tu fais...

la lessive.

Use faire to express temperature:
Il fait... (and add the number of degrees).

You are doing...

the laundry.

If you want to take your laundry to the laundromat, you would visit la blanchisserie or la lavarie automatique. A washing machine is translated as une machine à laver and a dryer is un séchoir.

Il fait...

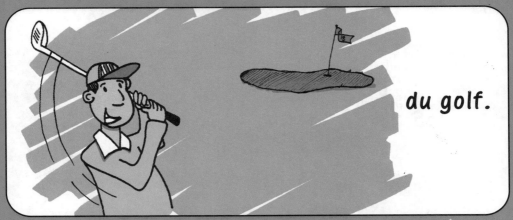

du golf.

When discussing the sports which you play, you can either use the verb jouer (to play) or the verb faire.

He plays...

golf.

To see a list of sports, check out Glossary Pages 216-217.

52

Nous ne faisons pas...

de basket-ball.

Another French/English cognate. Practice your pronunciation so that French speakers understand what you're referring to.

We don't play...

basketball.

Even though the verb faire is usually translated into English as to do or to make, it is also used when referring to playing sports.

Faites-vous...

la cuisine?

The verbs cuire and cuisiner means to cook. The cook is le cuisinier/la cuisinière. Kitchen is la cuisine.

Are you doing...

the cooking?

One of the many useful idiomatic expressions based on the verb faire is faites attention à... (Pay attention to...).

Je fais...

du thé.

Notice how faire can be translated as either to do, to make or to play. It's a versatile verb.

I am making...

some tea.

To say, I am making the tea, you simply use the definite article le (the) instead of the partitive article du (some).

Tu fais toujours...

tes devoirs.

Mastery Exercise: Je fais toujours mes devoirs.

You always do... (informal)

your homework.

Mastery Exercise: I always do my homework.

Ils font...

leur travail.

Mastery Exercise: Il fait son travail.

They do... (mixed)

their work.

Mastery Execise: He does his work.

Que faites-vous?

Mastery Exercise: Que fais-tu?

What are you doing? (plural)

Mastery Exercise: What are you doing?
(informal/singular)

Qu'est-ce qu'elles font?

Mastery Exercise: Qu'est-ce qu'elle fait?

What are they doing? (feminine)

Mastery Exercise: What is she doing?

Lesson 20

In this lesson you will learn...

- To express the concept of *which* and *what:*
  quel, quelle, quels, quelles.

- To express the concept of *which one(s)*
  and *what one(s)*: **lequel, laquelle, lesquels,
  lesquelles.**

Interrogative adjectives agree with the gender and the number of the noun they modify. Use the chart below to determine when to use which modifier.

		Masculine	**Feminine**
Singular	which/what	quel	quelle
Plural	which/what	quels	quelles

These adjectives are used to get more information by clarifying what a person is referring to. For example, **J'aime le film. Quel** (which) **film?**

Quel train est-ce que nous prenons?

Here is a nice example of how the interrogative adjective quel is used to obtain more information to clarify a situation.

What train are we taking?

Again, the number and gender of the noun described determine which form of quel, quelle, quels, or quelles to use.

Quelle est l'adresse de l'église?

Adresse is feminine and singular so the interrogative adjective quelle is chosen as the modifier.

71

What is the address of the church?

An important rule to remember is that être (to be) is the only verb that can separate an interrogative adjective from the noun it is modifying. For example, Quelle est l'adresse? (What is the address?)

Quels magazines est-ce que tu lis?

The word magazine is a French/English cognate, only the pronunciation differs.

Which magazines do you read? (informal)

To ask which newspaper someone reads, you would say,
Quel journal est-ce que tu lis?

Quelles chaussures est-ce que tu vas acheter?

The interrogative adjective quel can be used in exclamations and would be translated as what a...! for example: Quelle pagaille! (What a mess!)

75

Which shoes are you going to buy? (informal)

The use of quel, as in what a...!, can be used to describe your opinion of a meal. Quel repas délicieux! (What a delicious meal!) or Quelle bonne bière! (What good beer!)

Lequel préférez-vous?

The interrogative adjectives (quel, quelle, and quelles) can be changed into interrogative pronouns, simply by adding the definite article le, la, or les in front of the appropriate adjective. Le + quel = lequel, la + quelle = laquelle, les + quels/quelles = lesquels/lesquelles.

Which one do you want?

The interrogative pronouns lequel, laquelle, lesquels, and lesquelles are used when trying to determine what/which one(s) in a question.

Lesquelles de ces photos est-ce qu'il prend?

Just as with interrogative adjectives, interrogative pronouns must correspond in gender and number with the nouns they describe.

Which ones of these photos is he taking?

The verb prendre means to take and is used in the popular expression C'est à prendre ou à laisser (Take it or leave it).

Lesquelles de ces dames sont vos soeurs?

If you are deciding between two or more items in a shop, a salesperson would use an interrogative pronoun to learn your preference.

Which one(s) of these ladies are your sisters?

The interrogative pronoun is used to ask which one(s) of the noun/nouns specified.

Laquelle de ces
trois fleurs
préfèrez-vous?

Mastery Exercise: Lequel de ces trois livres
préfèrez-vous?

Which one of these three flowers do you prefer?

Mastery Exercise: Which one of these three books do you (formal) prefer?

84

Quel film
est ce que tu
recommandes?

Mastery Exercise:
Quels films est-ce que vous recommandez?

Which film do you (informal) **recommend?**

Mastery Exercise: Which films do you (plural) recommend?

Laquelle de ces trois valises est à toi?

The idiom être à means to belong to. The verb être is conjugated to match the given subject pronoun. Je suis à vous. (I am at your service.)

Which one of these three suitcases is yours?

When you are shopping, there are several useful phrases you should know: Je voudrais voir...(I would like to see...) and Y a-t-il des soldes? (Are there any sales?)

Lesson 21

In this lesson you will learn...

- To express the concepts of *this, that, these,* and *those;* **ce, cet, cette, ces.**

- To express the concepts of *here* **(ici)** and *there* **(là)** with the idea of *this, that, these,* and *those.*

- Add new Glossary Pages to your studies.

Use the chart on the following page as a guide to demonstrative adjectives.

Use the chart below as you work through the lesson:

ce	before all masculine singular nouns beginning with a consonant
cet	before all masculine singular nouns beginning with a vowel or silent h
cette	before all feminine, singular nouns
ces	before all plural nouns

The demonstrative adjectives **ce, cet,** and **cette** indicate *this, that;* **ces** indicates *these, those*.

Cette maison est formidable!

When using demonstrative adjectives you need to pay attention to the gender and the number of the noun you're describing. This phrase refers to one house (la maison), so cette is used.

This house is fantastic!

Knowing your demonstrative adjectives is very important when you're out shopping. It can help you to designate which product you're interested in.

Cet homme
mange beaucoup.

Here, the demonstrative adjective precedes a masculine
noun beginning with a silent h, so cet is used.

> That man
> eats a lot.

If you want to be more specific about which man you are referring to you could add a -ci (here) or a -là (there) after the given noun. Cet homme-çi means this man here and cet homme-là means that man there.

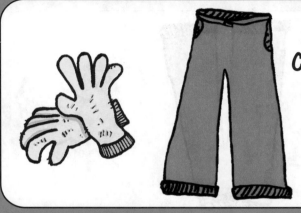

Ces gants et ces pantalons sont chouettes!

Notice how ces precedes any plural noun, regardless of its gender.

These gloves and those pants are great!

Chouette! (shoo-eht) is a term often used in French to express that something is great! or cool! If you like something, you can describe it as chouette.

Cet étudiant
étudie beaucoup.

Mastery exercise: Ces étudiants étudient beaucoup.

That student studies a lot.

Mastery Exercise: Those students study a lot.

Ce maillot de bain me plaît, mais cette robe de chambre ne me plaît pas.

Other useful expression you should know are: ça me plaît/I like it and ça me va/it suits me.

I like this bathing suit, but I don't like that robe.

The verb plaire means to please and it is used in the expressions s'il vous plaît and s'il te plaît (if you [polite/informal] please).

J'aime bien la robe que cette fille porte.

The verb porter means to wear or to carry and can be used in the expression porter son âge which means to look one's age.

I really like the dress that girl is wearing.

Always pay attention to the number and the gender of the noun a demonstrative adjective is modifying in order to use the correct form.

Je voudrais acheter cette pomme et ces bananes.

You must repeat demonstrative adjectives before each noun in a sentence.

I would like to buy this apple and those bananas.

To say I would like to buy this apple here, you would say *Je voudrais acheter cette pomme-ci.* Remember that -ci indicates here.

104

Vous devez trouver ces clés et son appareil-photo.

Mastery Exercise: Je vais trouver cette clé et cet appareil-photo.

You must find those keys and his camera.

Mastery Exercise: I am going to find that key and that camera.

Nous avons besoin de cet imperméable, ce pullover et ces chapeaux.

Mastery Exercise: J'ai besoin de ces imperméables, cette écharpe-là, et ce chapeau.

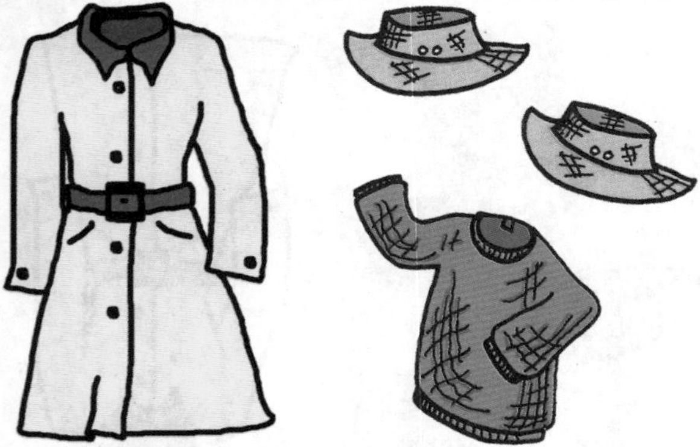

We need this raincoat, that sweater, and those hats.

Mastery Exercise: *I need those raincoats, that scarf there, and this hat.*

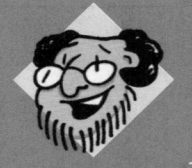

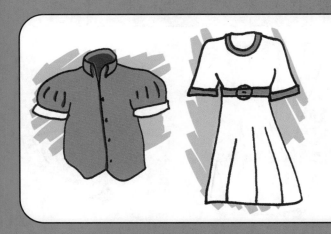

Elle préfère ce
chemisier-ci
mais
elle n'aime pas
cette robe-là.

Mastery Exercise: Elles préfèrent ces chemisiers-ci mais
ces robes-là sont trop grandes.

She prefers this blouse (here) but she doesn't like that dress (over there).

Mastery Exercise: They (all women) prefer those blouses (over here) but those dresses (over there) are too big.

110

Lesson 22

In this lesson you will learn...

- The present tense of regular verbs. The present tense is used to talk about actions people do on a habitual basis or plan to do in the near future.

Je parle français.	(I speak French.)
Je réponds à la question.	(I answer the question.)
Je finis maintenant.	(I'm finishing now.)

Use the chart on the following page as a guide to forming the present tense of regular verbs.

To form the present tense of regular verbs, simply drop the infinitive ending of the verb and add the following endings:

ER/parler	RE/répondre	IR/finir
je parle	je réponds	je finis
tu parles	tu réponds	tu finis
on/il/elle parle	on/il/elle répond	on/il/elle finit
nous parlons	nous répondons	nous finissons
vous parlez	vous répondez	vous finissez
ils/elles parlent	ils/elles répondent	ils/elles finissent

Note: Verbs not following a consistent pattern for change are presented in **Lesson 23.**

travailler

Je travaille beaucoup.

je	travaille
tu	<u>travailles</u>
on/il/elle	travaille
nous	travaillons
vous	travaillez
ils/elles	travaillent

All regular ER verbs express the je form in the same way.
Drop the -er ending and add -e.

to work

I work a lot.

Extra Practice:
**Do you (informal)
work a lot?**

You'll find the correct verb form for the Extra Practice sentences underlined in the chart on the other side of this page.

parler

Nous parlons anglais.

je	parle
tu	parles
on/il/elle	parle
nous	parlons
vous	<u>parlez</u>
ils/elles	parlent

To express the nous form of ER verbs, simply drop the -er ending and add -ons.

We speak English.

Extra Practice:

Do you speak English?

The present tense is used to express something you or someone else does habitually, such as eat, sleep, talk, etc.

fumer

Fumes-tu?

je	<u>fume</u>
tu	fumes
on/il/elle	fume
nous	fumons
vous	fumez
ils/elles	fument

All ER verbs express the tu form by dropping the -er ending and adding -es.

to smoke

Do you smoke?
(informal)

Extra Practice:
I don't smoke.

The present tense is also used to express things you don't do. *Je ne fume jamais!* (I never smoke!)

chanter

Les enfants chantent dans la chorale.

je	chante
tu	chantes
on/il/elle	chante
nous	<u>chantons</u>
vous	chantez
ils/elles	chantent

All ER verbs express they (ils, elles) by dropping the -er ending and adding -ent.

to sing

The children sing in the choir.

Extra Practice:
We sing in the choir.

The present tense also expresses actions in progress (the -ing form): Je parle./I am talking. Monique mange./Monique is eating.

étudier

Claire étudie à la bibliothèque.

j'	étudie
tu	étudies
on/il/elle	étudie
nous	étudions
vous	étudions
vous	étudiez
ils/elles	<u>étudient</u>

All verbs ending in ER express the il and elle forms by
dropping the -er ending and adding -e.

to study

Claire studies in the library.

Extra Practice:
They study in the library.

Doesn't it follow that what you study in school is called les études (studies)?

répondre

Je réponds au professeur en classe.

je	réponds
tu	réponds
on/il/elle	<u>répond</u>
nous	répondons
vous	répondez
ils/elles	répondent

All regular verbs that end in -re drop the -re and add -s for both **je** and **tu**.

to answer

I answer the professor in class.

Extra Practice:

He answers the professor in class.

Consistently reading French newspapers, books, or magazines is a great way to learn new words and practice what you know.

vendre

Il ne vend pas le journal au kiosque.

je	vends
tu	vends
on/il/elle	vend
nous	<u>vendons</u>
vous	vendez
ils/elles	vendent

The forms for il and elle for re verbs have no ending added and end in -d.

to sell

He doesn't sell the newspaper at the newsstand.

Extra Practice:

We don't sell the newspaper at the newsstand.

The stem of the verb carries the meaning. The ending of the verb identifies the person and the tense.

attendre

Philippe attend le bus à l'arrêt d'autobus.

j'	attends
tu	attends
on/il/elle	attend
nous	attendons
vous	attendez
ils/elles	<u>attendent</u>

Both ER and RE verbs express ils and elles by
dropping the -er or -re ending and adding -ent.

to wait

Philippe waits for the bus at the bus stop.

Extra Practice:
They wait for the bus at the bus stop.

Pay close attention to the -en sound in rendre and attendre. It's a nasal vowel sound that will come easier with practice.

finir

Pierre finit son travail à l'heure.

je	finis
tu	<u>finis</u>
on/il/elle	finit
nous	finissons
vous	finissez
ils/elles	finissent

Son travail (his work) uses a possessive adjective (his, her, my, your, our, etc.) Check out Lesson 6 for a review of possessive adjectives.

to finish

**Peter finishes his
work on time.**

Extra Practice:
**You (informal) finish
the task.**

Remember: All regular ER, RE and IR verbs follow a set
pattern which is the same for all verbs in that category.

choisir

Ils choisissent un repas différent chaque jour.

je	choisis
tu	choisis
on/il/elle	choisit
nous	<u>choisissons</u>
vous	choisissez
ils/elles	choisissent

Notice that the nous, vous, and ils/elles forms of the -ir verb add -iss to the verb stem.

to choose

**They choose a
different meal
every day.**

Extra Practice:
**We choose a different
meal every day.**

For a list of things you might find
in the restaurant, see Glossary Page 210.

Lesson 23

In this lesson you will...

• Learn to use common irregular verbs.

You've met some of the "good guys" (regular verbs), and even conjugated a few of their friends, who occasionally break out of the group and change the spelling in their stem.

In this lesson, you'll meet a few of the "bad guys," who refuse to conform to any pattern and insist on being irregular. Fortunately, they are used so often, you'll get to practice them often, because they are so important in French. The only real way to learn these verbs is to memorize them!

This is the final lesson on the present tense. Pay special attention to the following:

Master the verbs in each lesson! You cannot speak French effectively without knowing the French verb in all of its forms. Their importance cannot be overemphasized.

As you finish each group use the Mastery Sets on the CD as a self-test to identify areas where you may need practice. Review and practice if necessary so you have a strong foundation to build on.

lire

Je lis trois livres chaque semaine.

je	lis
tu	lis
on/il/elle	lit
nous	<u>lisons</u>
vous	lisez
il/elles	lisent

You may not realize how much you've already learned. The irregular verbs avoir, vouloir, devoir, aller, pouvoir, être and faire have been introduced in previous lessons.

to read

I read three books each week.

Extra Practice:

We read twelve books each month.

Although irregular verbs don't follow any set pattern, they are used all of the time, so you should memorize their endings as soon as you can.

Je vois le problème.

je	vois
tu	vois
on/il/elle	voit
nous	voyons
vous	<u>voyez</u>
ils/elles	voient

Notice that many irregular verbs have two different stems. Four forms: je, tu, il/elle, ils/elles, have one stem (voi) and nous and vous have another stem (voy).

to see

I see the problem.

Extra Practice:
Do you see the problem?

Another irregular French verb which is built from the verb voir (to see) is the verb recevoir (to receive, to get). Its stem for the four forms is reçoi- and for the two forms is recev-.

savoir

Je ne sais pas danser.

je	sais
tu	<u>sais</u>
on/il/elle	sait
nous	savons
vous	savez
ils/elles	savent

Savoir means to know a fact, or know how to do something. Savez-vous quelle heure est-il? (Do you know what time it is?)

to know (to know how)

I don't know how to dance.

Extra Practice:

Do you (informal) know how to dance?

Once you're comfortable with Lessons 17-24, it's time to test your mastery with the Week 3 CD.

connaître

Connaissez-vous Marie?

je	<u>connais</u>
tu	connais
on/il/elle	connaît
nous	connaissons
vous	connaissez
ils/elles	connaissent

Connaître means to know in the sense of being acquainted or being familiar with a person or place.

to know (to be acquainted with)

Do you know
Marie?

Extra Practice:
I don't know Marie.

See Glossary Pages 240-241 for more information
on when to use savoir and when to use connaître.

142

écrire

Écris-tu ton essai à ce moment?

j'	écris
tu	écris
on/il/elle	écrit
nous	écrivons
vous	écrivez
ils/elles	<u>écrivent</u>

Notice how no elision occurs between the second person singular (tu) and the third person singular (il/elle) subject pronouns and the conjugated form of écrire.

143

to write

Are you writing your essay right now? (informal)

Extra Practice:

Are they (all men) writing their essay right now?

A person who writes for a living is called un écrivain and the noun, writing, is translated as l'écriture.

prendre

Annick prend l'autobus devant le théâtre.

je	prends
tu	prends
on/il/elle	prend
nous	prenons
vous	prenez
ils/elles	<u>prennent</u>

Remember that verbs such as prendre are considered irregular because their forms don't fall into one of the three French verb families (er, ir, and re).

to take

Annick takes the bus in front of the theatre.

Extra Practice:
Jean-Claude and Claire take the bus in front of the theatre.

This irregular verb is used very often in French for talking about modes of transportation and traveling with your belongings.

mettre

Il met son gant sur la table.

je	mets
tu	mets
on/il/elle	met
nous	mettons
vous	mettez
ils/elles	<u>mettent</u>

The verb mettre can be used to describe putting on an article of clothing. Je mets mes chassures. (I put on my shoes.)

to put, to place (on)

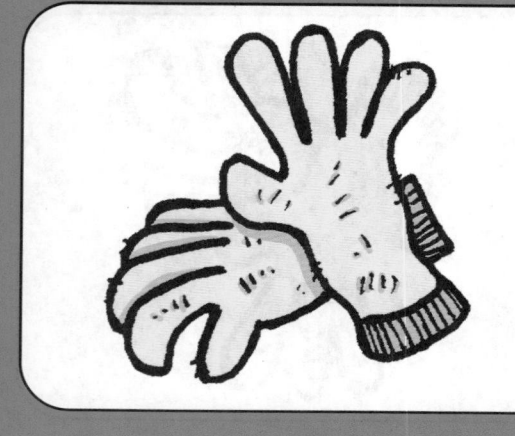

He puts his glove
on the table.

Extra Practice:

They (all females) put
their gloves on the table.

To set the table, you need to use the verb mettre.
Je mets la table. (I set the table.)

148

boire

Nous buvons du café chaque matin.

je	bois
tu	bois
on/il/elle	boit
nous	buvons
vous	buvez
ils/elles	<u>boivent</u>

The verb boire is frequently followed by the partitive article (part of the whole) to express *some* in the affirmative and *any* in the negative when speaking of drinks.

to drink

We drink some coffee every morning.

Extra Practice:

They don't drink coffee every morning.

The irregular verb *boire* is used very often during meals at home and in a restaurant.

dire

Vous dites beaucoup de choses intéressantes.

je	dis
tu	dis
on/il/elle	<u>dit</u>
nous	disons
vous	dites
ils/elles	disent

Compare the vous form of the verb faire (Lesson 19) to the vous form of the verb dire. This can help you remember both verbs better.

to say

You say a lot of interesting things.

Extra Practice:

He doesn't say a lot of interesting things.

Remember the present tense can be used to express the -ing form. Vous dites can be translated as you say or you are saying.

venir

Ils viennent à Paris chaque année.

je	viens
tu	viens
on/il/elle	vient
nous	<u>venons</u>
vous	venez
ils/elles	viennent

This irregular verb is used with geographical locations.
Use à before most cities.

to come

They come to Paris every year.

Extra Practice:

We come to Paris every year.

Note: Use the present tense form of venir de to express the concept of "to have just" done something. Je viens de visiter Paris. (I have just visited Paris.)

Lesson 24

In this lesson you will learn...

- To express commands. In order to give advice or tell someone to do something, you must learn to give commands (sometimes referred to as the imperative form).

Ouvrez la porte!	Open the door!
Apportez votre maillot de bain!	Bring your bathing suit!
Venez avec moi!	Come with me!

To express a command, simply drop the subject pronoun **vous** (formal) or **tu** (informal).

Come (formal) here!/Venez ici!   Come (informal) here!/Viens ici!

Infinitive	Command (vous)	Command (tu)
parler	Parlez!	Parle!
courrir	Courez!	Cours!
attendre	Attendez!	Attends!

Commands are also used occasionally with the subject pronoun nous. **Chantons!** (Let's sing!) See the notes on the pages in this lesson to learn how to express commands in the negative form and how to express commands with some commonly used irregular verbs.

parler

Parlez plus lentement s'il vous plaît!

Informal:
Parle/Ne parle pas

Drop the subject pronoun vous and use the vous form to tell someone to speak more slowly.

157

to speak

Speak slower
please!

Use informal commands to address family, friends,
coworkers, children and pets.

signer

Signez ici, s'il vous plaît!

Informal:

Signe/Ne signe pas

Note: When forming informal commands with -er verbs, drop the final -s in the tu form. Only -er verbs follow this rule.

to sign

Sign here, please!

To form formal negative commands, simply put ne before and pas after the formal form: Ne signez pas là! (Don't sign there!)

160

ouvrir

Ouvrez la porte!

Informal:
Ouvres/N'ouvres pas

Commands are often used when giving someone directions, as in Continuez tout droit! (Keep going straight ahead!)

to open

Open the door!

Using informal negative commands is the same as using formal ones - just add ne...pas: N'ouvres pas!

courir

Courez!

Informal:

Cours/ne cours pas

Another command commonly used with courir is the nous form, Courons! (Let's run!)

to run

Run!

An affirmative command is used to tell someone to do something. A negative command is when you tell them not to do something.

164

venir

Venez
avec moi!

Informal:
viens/ne viens pas

To tell a friend to come with you, use the informal
form and say: Viens avec moi! To tell him not to
come, say: Ne viens pas avec moi!

to come

Come with me!

Whether you're giving an affirmative command or a negative command, it's always nice to say s'il te plaît (informal) or s'il vous plaît (formal) at the end.

mettre

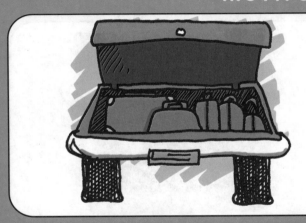

Mettons les valises dans le coffre!

Informal:
Mets/Ne mets pas

Before you pack the car, you might consider other modes of transportation. You could prendre (take) un taxi, le bus, or le métro.

to put

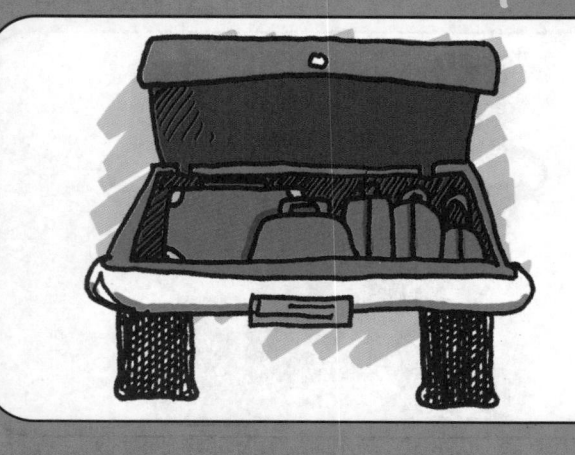

Let's put the suitcases in the trunk!

If you are going on a trip, don't forget l'essence (gas), l'assurance (insurance), and une carte (a map)!

attendre

Attendez-moi ici.

Informal:
Attends/N'attends pas

To tell someone not to wait for you here, say
Ne m'attendez pas ici.

to wait

Wait for me here!

You will learn all about how to use object pronouns (such as me, m') in Lesson 31.

suivre

Suivez cette voiture!

Informal:
Suis/Ne suis pas

Mastery Exercise: Suivez-moi!

to follow

Follow that car!

Mastery Exercise: Follow me!

apporter

Apportez votre maillot de bain.

Informal:
Apporte/N'apporte pas

Mastery Exercise: Apportons nos maillots de bain!

to bring

Bring your bathing suit.

Mastery Exercise: Let's bring our bathing suits!
(Remember, the nous form is used to express Let's...!)

aller

Allez à la porte numéro dix!

Informal:

Va/Ne va pas

Of course, some verbs are irregular in the command form. The informal command Va! (Go!) is one of them.

to go

Go to gate
number ten!

When you are ready to go with your group, say
Allons! (Let's go!)

Glossary

Glossary (cont.)

French Alphabet

a	ah	n	ehn
b	bay	o	oh
c	say	p	pay
d	day	q	kew
e	eh	r	ehr
f	ehf	s	ehs
g	zhay	t	tay
h	ahsh	u	ew
i	ee	v	vay
j	zhee	w	doo-bluh-vay
k	kah	x	eeks
l	ehl	y	ee-grehk
m	ehm	z	zehd

The French alphabet contains sounds not found in
English. Refer to Pages 181-185.

French Vowels

Vowel		Sounds like the...	French Word example:
a, à, â	(ah)	a as in ma	va (vah)
é, ai	(ay)	a as in pay	télé (tay-lay), j'ai (zhay)
e	(uh)	e as in the	je (zhuh)
è, ê, ei, ai	(eh)	e as in pet	très (treh), fête (feht), seize (sehz), fraise (frehz)
i, î, y, ui	(ee)	i as in tangerine	il (eel), île (eel), lycée (lee-say), nuit (nwee)
i + ll before a vowel	(y)	y as in you	gentille (zhahN-tee-y)
i + ll in certain words only	(eel)	ee as in eel	ville (veel), village (vee-lahzh) mille (meel), million (mee-lyahn), tranquille (trahN-keel)
o, ô, au, eau	(o)	o as in so	trop (troh), tôt (toh), au (oh), eau (oh)
o followed by a pronounced consonant	(oh)	o as in dove	donner (doh-nay)
ou, où, oû	(oo)	o as in tooth	toujours (too-zhoor)
oy, oi	(wah)	w as in wall	toi (twah), noir (nwahr)
u, û	(ew)	no equivalent - pucker lips	super (sew-pehr)

Sounds of French

Nasal sounds occur when a vowel is followed by a single M or a single N in the same syllable. To make a French nasal sound, plug your nose and then say the vowel sound out loud at the same time.

Nasal	Sounds Like	French Word
an, am, en, em	(ahN) on-w/accent on n	dans (dahN), lampe (lahNp)
in, im, ain, aim	(aN) an-w/accent on N	cinq (saNk), simple (saNpl),
	faim (faN)	
oin	(waN) wa in wag	coin (kwaN)
ien	(yaN) yan of hankie	bien (byaN)
on, om	(ohN) on as in tong	on (ohN),
		tomber (tohN-bay)
un, um	(uhN) un as in	un, (uhN),
	underwear	parfum (pahr-fuhN)

* Note that in the phonetic guide, if an n is capitalized (N), that is an indicator that the n or m needs to be pronounced with a nasal sound.

French Consonants

Consonant	Sounds Like	French Word
b, d, f, k, l, m,	same as in English	
c (hard before a, o, u, or consonant) qu, final q	(k) C as in carp	carte (kahrt), cinq (saNk)
c (soft before e, i, y), ç, s (at beginning of word and next to consonant), tion and x in given words	(s) cent	ce (suh), ça (sah), action (ahk-syohN), six (sees), dix (dees), soixant (swah-sahNt)
ch	(sh) ch as in machine	toucher (too-shay)
g (hard before a, o, u, or consonant), gu (before i, e, y)	(g) g as in goal	garçon (gahr-sohN), guide (geed)

French Consonants (cont.)

Consonant	Sounds like the...	French word
g (soft before e, i, y)	(*Zh*) as in treasure	**giraffe** (*Zhee-rahf*)
ge (softens **g** before a, o)		**âge** (*ahzh*),
j		**jupe** (*Zhewp*)
gn (ny)	*N* as in union	**Espagne** (*ehs-pah-nyuh*)
h	silent	**homme** (*ohm*), **heure**
(*uhr*)		
	or aspirated, no liaison	**haricot** (*hah-ree-koh*)
r	(*r*) gargle and say *r* at the same time	**merci** (*mehr-see*)
s (between vowels)	(*z*) Z as in zebra	**musique** (*mew-zeek*)
sion		
th	(*t*) t as in toe	**thé** (*tay*)
x	(*ks*) xc as in excellent	**extra** (*ehks-trah*)

Liaison, Elision, & Stress

Liaison (linking) refers to the linking of the final consonant of a word with the beginning vowel of the next word.

Example: vous arrivez (*voo zah-ree-vay*)

Elision (sliding) takes place when two pronounced vowel sounds are next to each other: one vowel sound is found at the end of the first word and the next vowel sound is found at the beginning of the second word. The first vowel sound is dropped and an apostrophe takes its place. The words are pronounced by sliding or contracting them together into one word. This gives spoken French its fluid sound.

Example: Je arrive ➡ J'arrive (*zhah-reev*)

Stress - all words in French are stressed evenly which helps give the language a more fluid cadence. Do not over-emphasize syllables, words or letters.

Time Elements

today	aujourd'hui	*oh-zhoor-dwee*
in the morning (a.m.)	du matin	*dew mah-taN*
in the afternoon (p.m.)	de l'après-midi	*duh-lah-preh mee-dee*
in the evening	du soir	*dew swahr*
this morning	ce matin	*suh mah-taN*
this afternoon	cet après-midi	*seht ah-preh mee-dee*
tonight	ce soir	*suh swahr*
on time	à temps	*ah tahN*
noon	midi	*mee-dee*
immediately	tout de suite	*toot sweet*
tomorrow	demain	*duh-man*
the day after tomorrow	après-demain	*ah-preh-duh-maN*
yesterday	hier	*yehr*
the day before yesterday	avant-hier	*ah-vahN tyehr*

Time Elements (cont.)

English	French	Pronunciation
last night	hier soir	*yehr swahr*
the week	la semaine	*lah suh-mehn*
last week	la semaine dernière	*lah suh-mehn dehr-nyehr*
each week	chaque semaine	*shahk suh-mehn*
next week	la semaine prochaine	*lah suh-mehn proh-shehn*
the weekend	le week-end	*luh week-end*
a moment	un moment	*uhN mo-mahn*
after	après	*ah-preh*
all the time	tout le temps	*too luh tahn*
always	toujours	*too-zhoor*
before	avant	*a-vahn*
during	pendant	*pahN-dahN*
early	de bonne heure	*duh boh nuhr*

Time Elements (cont.)

everyday	chaque jour	*shahk zhoor*
late	tard	*tahr*
later	plus tard	*plew tahr*
lots of times	beaucoup de temps	*bo-koo duh tahn*
never	jamais	*zhah-may*
now	maintenant	*mahN-tuh-nahN*
often	souvent	*soo-vahN*
once	une fois	*uhn fwah*
right now	en ce moment	*ahN suh moh-mahN*
seldom	rarement	*rahr-mahN*
since	depuis	*duh-pwee*
sometimes	quelquefois	*kehl-kuh-fwah*
soon	bientôt	*byan-to*
still	encore, toujours	*ahN-kohr, too-zhoor*
lately, recently	récemment	*ray-suh-mahN*
until	jusqu'à	*zhew-skah*

Weather

Quel temps fait-il? (What s the weather like?)
Weather and temperature are often expressed using the
present tense form of the verb **faire**.

It's sunny.	Il fait du soleil.	*eel feh dew soh-lehy*
It's cold	Il fait froid.	*eel feh frwah*
It's hot.	Il fait chaud.	*eel feh shoh*
It's cool.	Il fait frais.	*eel feh freh*
The weather's nice.	Il fait beau.	*eel feh boh*
The weather's bad.	Il fait mauvais.	*eel feh moh-veh*
How is the climate?	Comment est le climat?	*kohN-mahN eh luh klee-mah?*
It's clear.	Le ciel est clair.	*luh syehl eh klehr*

It's cloudy.	Le ciel est nuageux.	*luh syehl eh new-ah-zhuh*
It's overcast.	Le ciel est couvert.	*luh syehl eh koo-vehr*
It's raining.	Il pleut.	*eel pluh*
It's snowing.	Il neige.	*eel nehzh*
There is snow.	Il y a de la neige.	*eel yah duh lah nehzh*
There is rain.	Il y a de la pluie.	*eel yah duh lah plwee*
There are clouds.	Il y a des nuages.	*eel yah day new-ahzh*
There is a lot of wind.	Il y a beaucoup de vent.	*eel yah bo-koo dew vahN*
There are showers.	Il y a des giboulées.	*eel yah day zhee-boo-lay*
There is a rainbow.	Il y a un arc en ciel.	*eel yah uhN ahrk ahn syehl*

Temperature

The French use a Celsius (centigrade) thermometer to tell the temperature.

To convert Fahrenheit to Celsius, subtract 32 degrees, multiply by 5 and divide by 9.

To convert Celsius to Fahrenheit, multiply by 9, divide by 5 and add 32 degrees.

Seasons & The Universe

seasons	les saisons	*lay say-zohN*
spring	le printemps	*luh praN-tahN*
summer	l'été	*lay-tay*
fall	l'automne	*lo-tohn*
winter	l'hiver	*lee-vehr*
Universe	l'univers	*lew-nee-vehr*
earth	la terre	*lah tehr*
sun	le soleil	*luh soh-lehy*
moon	la lune	*lah lewn*
stars	les étoiles	*lay zay-twahl*
world	le monde	*luh mohNd*
galaxy	la galaxie	*lah gah-lah-ksee*

People

adult	l'adulte	lah-dewlt
teenager	la jeune, l'adolescent(e)	lah zhuhn
man	l'homme	luhm
woman	la femme	lah fahm
Mr.	Monsieur	muh-syuh
Mrs.	Madame	mah-dahm
lady	la dame	lah dahm
gentleman	le monsieur	luh muh-syuh
boyfriend	le petit ami	luh puh-tee tah-mee
girlfriend	la petite amie	lah puh-tee tah-mee
Miss	Mademoiselle	mahd-mwah-zehl

People (cont.)

enemy	l'ennemi(e)	lehn-nuh-mee
friend	l'ami(e)	lah-mee
group	le groupe	luh groop
parents	les parents	lay pah-rahN
people	les gens	lay zhahN
person	la personne	lah pehr-sohn
anyone	n'importe qui	naN-pohrt kee
everyone	tout le monde	too luh mohNd
no one	personne	pehr-sohn
someone	quelqu'un	kehl-kuhN

The expression no one/nobody should be followed by
"ne" before the verb of the sentence.
For example: Personne n'est là. (No one is there)

Professions & Occupations

architect	l'architecte	*l'ahr-shee-tehkt*
banker	le banquier	*luh bahn-kyeh*
carpenter	le charpentier	*luh shahr-pahN-tyeh*
dentist	le dentiste	*luh dahN-teest*
doctor	le docteur, le médecin	*luh dohk-tuhr;*
		luh mayd-saN
electrician	l'électricien	*lay-lehk-tree-syan*
engineer	l'ingénieur	*laN-zhay-nyuhr*
farmer	le fermier	*luh fehr-myeh*

When discussing a profession, the indefinite article "un(e)"
is not used unless the profession is described by an adjective.
For example: Je suis dentiste. (I am a dentist.) But: Je suis
un bon dentiste. (I am a good dentist.)

firefighter	le pompier	*luh pohN-pyeh*
gardener	le jardinier	*luh zhahr-daN-nyeh*
lawyer	l'avocat	*lah-voh-kah*
mechanic	le mecanicien	*luh may-kah-nee-syaN*
pharmacist	le pharmacien	*luh fahr-mah-syan*
plumber	le plombier	*luh plohN-myeh*
police officer	l'agent de police	*lah-zahN duh poh-lees*
professor	le professeur	*luh pro-feh-suhr*
reporter	le/la journaliste	*luh/lah zhoor-nah-leest*
secretary	le/la secrétaire	*luh/lah seh-kray-tehr*
student	l'étudiant	*lay-tew-dyahN*
teacher	l'instituteur	*laN-stee-tew-tuhr*

The Body

the body	le corps	*luh kohr*
arm	le bras	*luh brah*
back	le dos	*luh do*
bones	les os	*layz o*
cheek	la joue	*lah zhoo*
chest	la poitrine	*lah pwah-treen*
chin	le menton	*luh mahN-tohN*
ear	l'oreille (f.)	*loh-rehy*
elbow	le coude	*luh kood*
eye/eyes	l'oeil (m.)/les yeux	*luhy/lay zhuh*
face	le visage	*luh vee-zahzh*
finger	le doigt	*luh dwah*

The Body (cont.)

foot	le pied	*luh pyay*
hair	les cheveux	*lay shuh-vuh*
hand	la main	*lah-maN*
head	la tête	*lah teht*
knee	le genou	*luh zhuh-noo*
leg	la jambe	*lah zhahNb*
mouth	la bouche	*lah boosh*
neck	le cou	*luh koo*
nose	le nez	*luh nay*
shoulder	l'épaule	*lay-pohl*
stomach	l'estomac (m.) /le ventre	*lay-stoh-mah, luh vahNtr*
toe	l'orteil (m.)	*lohr-tehy*

I Need a Doctor!

I need a doctor!	J'ai besoin d'un médecin!	*Zhay buh-zwan duhn mayd-saN*
I have...	J'ai...	*zhai*
a backache	mal au dos	*mahl o do*
a broken bone	une fracture	*ewn frahk-tewr*
a cold	un rhume	*uhN rewm*
a fever	de la fièvre	*duh la fyehvr*
the flu	la grippe	*lah greep*
a headache	mal à la tête	*mahl ah la teht*
a sore throat	mal à la gorge	*mahl ah lah gohrzh*
a stomach ache	mal au ventre	*mahl o vahNtr*
a toothache	mal aux dents	*mahl o dahn*
a burn	une brûlure	*ewn brew-lewr*

I Need a Doctor! (cont.)

a cut	une coupure	*ewn koo-pewr*
nausea	des nausées	*day no-zay*
a sprain	une foulure	*ewn foo-lewr*
a wound	une blessure	*ewn bleh-sewr*
accident	un accident	*uhN ahk-see-dahN*
appointment	un rendez-vous	*uhN rahN-day-voo*
clinic	service de consultation	*sehr-vees duh kohN-sewl-tah-syohN*
emergency	cas urgent	*kah-oor-zhahN*
examination	un examen	*uhN eks-zah-mahN*
health	la santé	*lah sahN-tay*
hospital	l'hôpital	*loh-pee-tahl*

Pharmacy

adhesive bandage	pansement adhésif	*pahNs-mahN ahd-hay-seef*
alcohol	de l'alcool	*duh lahl-kohl*
antiseptic	un antiseptique	*uhN nahN-tee-sehp-teek*
antacid	un anti-acide	*uhN nahN-tee ah-seed*
aspirins	des aspirines	*day zah-spee-reen*
bandage	des pansements (m.)	*day pahNs-mahN*
cotton	du coton de l'ouate	*dew koh-tohN duh lwaht*
gauze	de la gaze	*duh la gahz*
medicine	des médicaments	*day may-dee-kah-mahN*

pills	des pilules (f.)	*day pee-lewl*
prescription	une ordonnance	*ewn ohr-doh-nahNs*
razor	un rasoir	*uhN rah-zwahr*
razor blade	des lames de rasoir	*day lahm duh rah-zwahr*
shampoo	du shampooing	*dew shahN-pwaN*
thermometer	un thermomètre	*uhN tehr-mo-mehtr*
toothbrush	une brosse à dents	*ewn brohs ah dahN*
toothpaste	de la pâte dentifrice	*duh lah paht dahN-tee-frees*
vitamins	des vitamines	*day vee-tah-meen*

In The Kitchen

English	French	Pronunciation
in the kitchen	à la cuisine	*ah lah kwee-zeen*
the cook	un cuisinier	*uhN kwee-zee-nyay*
apron	un tablier	*uhN tah-blee-yay*
coffee pot	une cafetière	*ewn kah-fay-tee-yehr*
dishes	la vaisselle	*lah veh-sehl*
pan (frying)	une poêle à frire	*ewn pwahl ah freer*
pot	une marmite	*ewn mahr-meet*
pitcher	une cruche	*ewn krewsh*
silverware	l'argenterie (f.)	*lahr-zhahN-tuh-ree*
saucepan	une casserole	*ewn kah-suh-rohl*
tea kettle	une bouilloire	*ewn boo-eey-wahr*
tray	un plateau	*uhN plah-to*

Appliances

blender	un mixeur	*uhN meeks-uhr*
can opener	l'ouvre-boîtes (m.)	*loo-vruh-bwaht*
dishwasher	un lave-vaisselle	*uhN lahv veh-sehl*
dryer	un séchoir	*uhN say-shwahr*
freezer	un congélateur	*uhN kohN-zhay-lah-tuhr*
mixer	un mixeur	*uhN meeks-uhr*
oven	un four	*uhN foor*
refrigerator	un réfrigérateur	*uhN ray-free-zhay-rah-tuhr*
stove	une cuisinière	*ewn kwee-zeen-yehr*
vacuum cleaner	un aspirateur	*uhN ah-spee-rah-tuhr*
washing machine	une machine à laver	*ewn mah-sheen ah lah-vay*

The Laundry

the laundry	la blanchisserie	*lah blahN-shees-ree*
broom	un balai	*uhN bah-lay*
detergent	le détergent	*luh day-tuhr-zahN*
dirty clothes	la lessive	*lah leh-seev*
hangers	des cintres	*day saNtr*
iron	un fer à repasser	*uhN fehr ah ruh-pah-say*
ironing board	la planche à repasser	*lah plahNsh ah ruh-pah-say*
mop	un balai laveur	*uhn bah-lay lah-vuhr*
sponge	une éponge	*ewn ay-pohNzh*
stain	une tache	*ewn tahsh*
starch	l'amidon (m.)	*lah-mee-dohn*

Patio & Garden

butterfly	le papillon	*luh pah-pee-yohN*
flowers	les fleurs	*lay fluhr*
fly	la mouche	*lah moosh*
fly swatter	la tapette	*lah tah-peht*
garden	le jardin	*luh zhahr-daN*
grass	l'herbe (f.)	*lehrb*
insects	les insectes (m.)	*lay zaN-sehkt*
lawn mower	la tondeuse	*lah tohn-dewz*
pool	la piscine	*lah pee-seen*
shade	l'ombre (f.)	*lohNbr*
tree	l'arbre (m.)	*lahrbr*

Transportation

ambulance	l'ambulance (f.)	*lahN-bew-lahNs*
airplane	l'avion (m.)	*lah-vyohn*
baby carriage	la voiture d'enfant	*lah vwah-tewr dahn-fahn*
bicycle	la bicyclette	*lah bee-see-kleht*
boat	le bateau	*luh bah-to*
bus	le bus	*luh bews*
scooter	la moto	*luh moh-to*
canoe	le canöe	*luh kah-noh*
captain	le capitaine	*luh kahp-tehn*
car	la voiture	*lah vwah-tewr*
cruise ship	la croisière	*lah kwah-zee-yehr*
fire engine	la voiture de pompiers	*lah vwah-tewr duh pohN-pyeh*

Transportation (cont.)

helicopter	l'hélicoptère (m.)	*lay-lee-kohp-tehr*
motorcycle	la motocyclette	*lah moh-to-see-kleht*
rowboat	le canot à rames	*luh kah-no-ah-rahm*
sailboat	le voilier	*luh vwah-lyay*
school bus	car de ramassage scolaire	*kahr duh rah-mah-sahzh skoh-lehr*
scooter	le scooter	*luh skootur*
subway	le métro	*luh may-tro*
taxi	le taxi	*luh tahk-see*
tow truck	la dépanneuse	*lah day-pahN-ews*
train	le train	*luh traN*
truck	le camion	*luh kah-mee-ohN*
van	la camionnette	*lah kah-mee-ohN-et*

The Car

battery	la batterie	*lah bah-tree*
brakes	les freins (m.)	*lay fraN*
brake light	le feu de stop	*luh fuh duh stahp*
bumper	le pare-choc	*luh pahr-shohk*
carburetor	le carburateur	*luh kahr-bew-rah-tuhr*
engine	le moteur	*luh moh-tuhr*
fender	l'aile (f.)	*lehl*
flat tire	le pneu à plat	*luh pnuh a plah*
gas tank	le réservoir à essence	*luh ray-sehr-vwahr ah eh-sahNs*
gauge	l'indicateur (m.)	*lahN N-dee-kah-tuhr*
headlight	le feu	*luh fuh*

The Car (cont.)

hood	le capot	*luh kah-po*
horn	le klaxon	*luh klahk-sohN*
ignition	l'allumage	*lah-lew-mahzh*
rearview mirror	le rétroviseur	*luh ray-troh-vee-zuhr*
seat	la siège	*lah see-ehzh*
spare tire	le pneu de rechange	*luh pnuh duh ruh-shanhzh*
steering wheel	le volant	*luh voh-lahN*
trunk	le coffre	*luh kohfr*
windshield	le pare-brise	*luh pahr-breez*
windshield wiper	l'essuie-glace (m.)	*lah-swee glahs*

The Restaurant

appetizers	**les hors-d'oeuvre**	*lay zohr-doohvr*
bar	**le bar**	*luh bahr*
breakfast	**le petit déjeuner**	*luh puh-tee day-zhoo-nay*
check	**l'addition (f.)**	*lah dee-syohN*
cook	**le cuisinier**	*luh kwee-zeen-nyay*
dinner	**le dîner**	*luh dee-nay*
lunch	**le déjeuner**	*luh day-zhuh-nay*
menu	**le menu**	*luh meh-new*
reservation	**la réservation**	*lah ray-sehr-vah-syohN*
snack/tea	**le goûter**	*luh goo-tay*
tip	**le pourboire**	*luh poor-bwahr*
waiter	**le serveur/ le garçon**	*luh suhr-vuhr/ luh gahr-sohN*

Who's Calling

Hello!	Allô!
Hello!	Bonjour!
Who's calling?	Qui est à l'appareil?
I would like to speak to...	Je voudrais parler à...
Can I speak with...?	Est-ce que je peux parler à...?
Is Marie in?	Marie est là?
When will she return?	Quand sera-t-elle de retour?
Don't hang up!	Ne quittez pas!
May I leave a message?	Pourrais-je laisser un message?
I'll call back...	Je vais rappeler...
Call me back...	Rappelez-moi...

In The Hotel

Where is...?	Où est...?	oo ay
the bellhop	le concierge	luh kohN-syehrzh
the doorman	le portier	luh pohr-tyay
the elevator	l'ascenseur (m.)	lah-sahN-suhr
the floor	l'étage*	lay-tazh
the key	la clé	lah klay
the maid	la bonne	lah buhn
the manager	le gérant	luh zhay-rahN
the pool	la piscine	lah pee-seen

*The word étage (floor) refers to floors above the ground.
The ground floor is called le rez-de-chaussée.

In The Hotel (cont.)

I need...	J'ai besoin de...	zhay buh-zwaN duh
a blanket	une couverture	ewn koo-vehr-tewr
a pillow	un oreiller	uhN noh-reh-yay
a room	une chambre	ewn shahNbr
a single room	une chambre à un	ewn shahNbr ah uhn
a double room	une chambre à deux	ewn shahNbr ah duh
a sheet	un drap	uhN drah
a shower	une douche	ewn doosh
more ice	plus de glaçons (m.)	plew duh glah-sohN
more soap	plus de savon	plew duh sah-vohn
more towels	plus de serviettes	plew duh sehr-vyeht
toilet paper	le papier hygiénique	luh pah-pyay ee-zhyay-neek

In The Classroom

the classroom	**la salle de classe**	*lah sahl duh klahs*
books	**les livres (m.)**	*lay leevr*
chalk	**la craie**	*lah kray*
crayon	**le crayon de couleur**	*luh kray-ohN duh koo-luhr*
homework	**les devoirs (m.)**	*lay day-vwahr*
map	**la carte**	*lah kahrt*
notebook	**le cahier**	*luh kah-yay*
problems	**les problèmes (m.)**	*lay proh-blehm*
pupil's desk	**le bureau d'élève**	*luh bew-roh day-lehv*
student	**l'étudiant (m.) / l'élève**	*lay-tew-dee-ahN/lay lehv*
teacher	**le professeur / l'instituteur (m.)**	*luh proh-feh-sur/ laN-stee-too-tuhr*

Games & Toys

toys	les jouets (m.)	lay zhoo-ay
cards	les cartes (f.)	lay kahrt
checkers	le jeu de dames (m.)	luh zhuh duh dahm
chess	les échecs (m.)	lay-shek
doll	la poupée	lah poo-pay
games	les jeux (m.)	lay zhuh
kite	le cerf-volant	luh sehrf-voh-lahN
marbles	les billes (f.)	lay beel
puzzle	le casse-tête, le puzzle	lah kahs-teht, luh pewzl
slide	le toboggan	luh toh-boh-gahN
swing	la balançoire	lah bah-lahN-swahr

Sports & Equipment

ball	la balle	lah bahl
baseball	du base-ball	dew bays-bohl
bat	la batte	lah baht
basketball	du basket-ball	dew bahs-keht bohl
boxing	la boxe	lah bohks
bowling	le bowling	luh boh-leeng
football	du football américain	dew foot-bohl ah-may-ree-kaN
golf	du golf	dew gohlf
golf clubs	les clubs de golf (m.)	lay klewb duh gohlf
gym	le gymnase	luh zheem-nahz
hockey	du hockey	dew oh-kee

Sports & Equipment (cont.)

horseback riding	de l'équitation (f.)	duh lay-kee-tay-syohN
mitt	le gant	luh gahN
racket	la raquette	lah rah-keht
racquetball	du raquette-ball	dew rah-keht-bohl
umpire	l'arbitre (m.)	lahr-beetr
skating	du patin	dew pah-taN
skates	les patins	lay pah-taN
soccer	du football	dew foot-bohl
swimming	de la natation	duh la nah-tah-syohN
team	l'équipe (f.)	lay keep
tennis	du tennis	dew teh-nees
volleyball	du volley-ball	dew voh-lee bohl

Action Words

abandon, to	abandonner	anger, to	se fâcher
absorb, to	absorber	annul, to	annuler
accept, to	accepter	answer, to	répondre
acquire, to	acquérir	appear, to	apparaître
add, to	ajouter	argue, to	se disputer
adhere, to	adhérer	arrange, to	arranger
adjust, to	s'adapter à	arrest, to	arrêter
advance, to	avancer	ask, to	demander
advise, to	conseiller	ask for, to	demander
affirm, to	affirmer	assist, to	aider
agree, to	consentir	attack, to	attaquer
analyze, to	analyser	attend, to	assister

Action Words (cont.)

attract, to	attirer	bet, to	parier
authorize, to	autoriser	bite, to	mordre
be, to	être	blame, to	blâmer
be, to	exister	bleed, to	saigner
be able, to	pouvoir	block, to	bloquer
be born, to	naître	blow, to	souffler
be missing, to	avoir disparu	boil, to	bouillir
be worth, to	valoir	bother, to	ennuyer
beat, to	battre	break, to	casser
beg, to	mendier	breathe, to	respirer
begin, to	commencer	bring, to	amener
believe, to	croire	build, to	bâtir
bend, to	courber	burn, to	brûler

Action Words (cont.)

buy, to	acheter	climb, to	monter
call, to	appeler	close, to	fermer
calm, to	calmer	come, to	venir
carry, to	porter	come in, to	entrer
catch, to	attraper	compete, to	concourir
cause, to	causer	complain, to	se plaindre
celebrate, to	célébrer	concede, to	concéder
change, to	changer	conceive, to	concevoir
charge, to	charger	conclude, to	conclure
chat, to	bavarder	confuse, to	confondre
check, to	vérifier	consent, to	consentir
choose, to	choisir	conserve, to	conserver
clean, to	nettoyer	consider, to	considérer

Action Words (cont.)

consist, to	consister	cry, to	pleurer
consult, to	consulter	cure, to	guérir
contain, to	contenir	cut, to	couper
contribute, to	contribuer	dance, to	danser
control, to	se faire obéir de	decide, to	décider
converse, to	converser	declare, to	déclarer
convince, to	convaincre	dedicate, to	dédier
cook, to	cuire	defend, to	défendre
correct, to	corriger	delay, to	retarder
cost, to	coûter	deliver, to	remettre, livrer
cough, to	tousser	deny, to	nier
crash, to	s'écraser	depend, to	dépendre
cross, to	traverser	describe, to	décrire

Action Words (cont.)

deserve, to	valoir, mériter	do (make), to	faire
desire, to	désirer	draw, to	dessiner
destroy, to	détruire	dream, to	rêver
detain, to	retenir	drink, to	boire
die, to	mourir	drive, to	conduire
dig, to	creuser	dry, to	sécher
direct, to	diriger	earn, to	gagner
discover, to	découvrir	eat, to	manger
discuss, to	discuter	eliminate, to	éliminer
dissolve, to	dissoudre	empty, to	vider
distract, to	distraire	end, to	finir
distribute, to	distribuer	enter, to	entrer
divide, to	diviser		

Action Words (cont.)

escape, to	échapper	fight, to	se battre
evacuate, to	évacuer	fill, to	remplir
evaluate, to	évaluer	find, to	trouver
enjoy, to	aimer	find out, to	découvrir
examine, to	examiner	finish, to	finir
exchange, to	échanger	fish, to	pêcher
exist, to	exister	fit, to	aller à
explain, to	expliquer	fix, to	fixer
explore, to	explorer	flee, to	fuir
fall, to	tomber	fly, to	voler
fear, to	craindre	follow, to	suivre
feed, to	nourrir	forbid, to	défendre
feel, to	sentir	forget, to	oublier

Action Words (cont.)

forgive, to	pardonner	greet, to	accueillir
form, to	former	grow, to	grandir
freeze, to	geler (move up)	guess, to	deviner
frighten, to	effrayer	hang, to	pendre
fulfill, to	accomplir, réaliser	happen, to	se passer
function, to	fonctionner	hate, to	haïr
get, to	avoir, obtenir	have, to	avoir
get down, to	descendre	have to, to	devoir
get near, to	approcher	hear, to	entendre
give, to	donner	help, to	aider
go, to	aller	hide, to	cacher
go out, to	sortir	hire, to	louer
grab, to	saisir	hit, to	battre

Action Words (cont.)

hold, to	tenir	install, to	installer
hug, to	étreindre	interpret, to	interpréter
to imagine, to	imaginer	introduce, to	introduire
include, to	inclure	invest, to	placer
increase, to	grandir	investigate, to	scruter
indicate, to	indiquer	invite, to	inviter
inflate, to	gonfler	judge, to	juger
inform, to	informer	jump, to	sauter
inhibit, to	dominer	keep, to	garder
injure, to	blesser	kick, to	donner un coup de pied
insert, to	insérer	kiss, to	embrasser
inspect, to	inspecter	know, to	connaître
insure, to	s'assurer, assurer	know (how), to	savoir

Action Words (cont.)

lay, to	mettre, poser, étendre	look for, to	chercher
lead, to	mener	loosen, to	défaire
learn, to	apprendre	lose, to	perdre
leave, to	sortir de, laisser, quitter, partir de	love, to	aimer
lend, to	prêter	maintain, to	maintenir
let, to	laisser, permettre	make, to	faire
lie, to	mentir	mean, to	vouloir dire, signifier
lift, to	lever	measure, to	mesurer
light, to	allumer	meet, to	rencontrer
like, to	aimer	melt, to	fondre
listen, to	écouter	move, to	bouger, déplacer
live, to	vivre	name, to	appeler/nommer
look at, to	regarder	need, to	avoir besoin de

Action Words (cont.)

neglect, to	négliger	open, to	ouvrir
note, to	noter	operate, to	opérer
notify, to	signaler	oppose, to	s'opposer à
obey, to	obéir	order, to	ordonner, commander
oblige, to	obliger	owe, to	devoir
observe, to	remarquer, observer	park, to	garer, stationner
obstruct, to	boucher, bloquer	pay, to	payer
obtain, to	obtenir	perceive, to	percevoir
occupy, to	occuper	permit, to	permettre
occur, to	avoir lieu, arriver	persist, to	persister
offend, to	offenser, choquer	pick up, to	ramasser
offer, to	offrir	plant, to	planter
omit, to	omettre	play, to	jouer

Action Words (cont.)

plug in, to	brancher	propose, to	proposer
point, to	pointer, montrer	protect, to	protéger
practice, to	s'entraîner, s'exercer	prove, to	prouver
pray, to	prier	pull, to	tirer
prefer, to	préférer	push, to	pousser
prepare, to	préparer	put, to	mettre, placer, poser
present, to	présenter	quit, to	quitter, arrêter
prevent, to	empêcher	reach, to	atteindre, arriver
proceed, to	aller, avancer	read, to	lire
progress, to	aller, avancer	receive, to	recevoir
prohibit, to	défendre, interdire	recognize,	to reconnaître
promise, to	promettre	recover, to	reprendre, retrouver
		reduce, to	réduire

Action Words (cont.)

refer, to	soumettre, parler	rob, to	dévaliser, voler
remember, to	se rappeler, se souvenir	run, to	courir
rent, to	louer	save, to	sauver
repair, to	réparer	say, to	dire
repeat, to	répéter	scratch, to	gratter
require, to	exiger	search, to	chercher
resolve, to	résoudre	see, to	voir
respect, to	respecter	seem, to	paraître, sembler
respond, to	répondre	seize, to	saisir
rest, to	se reposer	sell, to	vendre
retire, to	se retirer	send, to	envoyer
return, to	rentrer, retourner	separate, to	séparer
ride, to	monter à	serve, to	servir

Action Words (cont.)

set, to	poser, mettre	stay, to	rester
sew, to	coudre	stick, to	coller, tenir
shake, to	trembler, agiter	stop, to	arrêter
shine, to	luire, briller	study, to	étudier
shout, to	crier	suppose, to	supposer
show, to	montrer	swallow, to	avaler
sign, to	signer	swim, to	nager
sing, to	chanter	take, to	prendre
sleep, to	dormir	take care of, to	s'occuper de
smoke, to	fumer	to take off, to	enlever
snow, to	neiger	take out, to	enlever, sortir
speak, to	parler	teach, to	enseigner
spend, to (money)	dépenser	tell, to	dire
spend, to (time)	passer		

Action Words (cont.)

thank, to	remercier	visit, to	visiter, rendre visite à
think, to	penser	vote, to	voter
throw, to	jeter	wait, to	attendre
tire, to	fatiguer	walk, to	marcher
touch, to	toucher	want, to	vouloir
translate, to	traduire	wash, to	laver
travel, to	voyager	watch, to	regarder
try, to	essayer	win, to	gagner
turn, to	tourner	wish, to	souhaiter
turn on, to	allumer	work, to	travailler
turn off, to	fermer	worry, to	inquiéter
understand, to	comprendre	write, to	écrire
use, to	employer, utiliser		

Reflexive Verbs

bathe oneself, to	se baigner
be called/named, to	s'appeler
become angry, to	se fâcher
begin, to	se mettre à
break, to (body part)	se casser
brush (hair, teeth), to	se brosser
do one's hair, to	se coiffer
feel, to	se sentir
get dressed, to	s'habiller
get up, to	se lever
go to bed, to	se coucher
have fun, to	s'amuser
hurry, to	se dépêcher

Reflexive Verbs

hurt oneself, to	se blesser
remember, to	se souvenir
rest, to	se reposer
shave, to	se raser
sit down, to	s'asseoir
stop (oneself), to	s'arrêter
take a walk, to	se promener
undress, to	se déshabiller
wake up, to	se réveiller
wash (oneself), to	se laver
wonder, to	se demander
worry about, to	s'inquiéter de

Expressions with Avoir

avoir l'occasion de	to have the opportunity to
avoir de la chance	to be lucky
avoir l'habitude de	to be accustomed to
avoir l'intention de	to intend to
avoir le temps de	to have the time to
avoir lieu	to take place
avoir besoin (de)	to need
avoir chaud	to be hot (person)
avoir envie (de)	to need, to want
avoir faim	to be hungry
avoir froid	to be cold (person)
avoir honte	to be ashamed (of)
avoir l'air de (+ adjective)	to seem, look as if
avoir à	to have to

More Expressions with Avoir

avoir mal à	to have an ache in
avoir peur (de)	to be afraid (of)
avoir quelque chose	to have something wrong
avoir raison	to be right
avoir soif	to be thirsty
avoir sommeil	to be sleepy
avoir tort	to be wrong
avoir... ans	to be...years old
avoir le droit de	to have the right to
avoir du chien	to be alluring, sexy

Expressions with Faire

faire attention (à…)	to pay attention (to…)
faire des achats (emplettes)	to go shopping
faire des courses	to do errands (shop)
faire exprès	to do on purpose
faire la connaissance de	to meet, become acquainted with
faire la queue	to stand in line
faire une partie de	to play a game of
faire une promenade	to take a walk
faire un voyage	to take a trip
faire venir	to send for
faire de votre mieux	to do your best
faire des siennes	to be up to one's old tricks
faire voir	to show

Expressions with Être & Faire

être à	to belong to
être d'accord (avec)	to agree (with)
être de retour	to be back
être en train de (+ infinitive)	to be in the act of, busy
être sur le point de (+ infinitive)	to be on the verge of
faire mal	to hurt
faire savoir	to inform
Il fait beau/froid.	It's beautiful/cold.
Il fait du soleil/du vent.	It's sunny/windy.
Il fait jour/nuit.	It's daytime/nightime.

Qu'est-ce que...?

Qu'est-ce qu'il y a?	What's there?/What's wrong?
Qu'est-ce que cela veut dire?	What does it mean?
Qu'est-ce que vous avez dit?	What did you say?
Qu'est-ce que vous faîtes?	What are you doing?
Quoi de neuf?	What's new?
Qu'est-ce que se passe?	What's up? What's happening?
Qu'est-ce que c'est?	What is it?
Qu'est-ce que vous voulez?	What do you want?
Qu'est-ce que c'est que ça?	What is this/that?

Quel? / Lequel?

Lequel?	Which one?
Lesquels?	Which ones?
Quel est votre nom?	What is your name?
Quel est votre nom de famille?	What is your last name?
Quelle est votre addresse?	What is your address?
Quel est votre numéro de téléphone?	What is your telephone number?
Lequel est à vous?	Which one is yours?
Lequel est-ce que vous aimez?	Which one would you like?
Lequel est-il?	Which one is it?
Quelle est la date aujourd'hui?	What is the date today?
Quel dommage!	Too bad!
Quelle heure est-il?	What time is it?

Savoir

Use *savoir* (to know) to express knowing how to do things and knowing facts. *Savoir* is not used in relation to knowing a person, an animal, a place, or a concrete object.

How to do things

Je sais jouer le violon.
I know how to play the violin.

Nous savons parler français.

We know how to speak French.

Knowing Facts

Il sait son nom.
He knows his/her name.

Vous savez où se trouve les toilettes.

You know where the toilets are located.

Connaître

Use *connaître* (to know) to express familiarity with a person, a place, a thing, or an idea. Use the verb *connaître* when you can substitute "to know" with "to be aquainted with."

A person
Je connais Sarah.
I know Sarah.

A concrete object
Vous connaissez ces fleurs.
You know about these flowers.

An animal.
Il connaît les oiseaux.
He knows about birds.

A place
Nous connaissons Paris.
We know Paris.

This & That

Use the chart below to choose the correct form of this, that, *those* and *those*. Demonstrative adjectives precede the nouns they modify and correspond to the number and gender of the noun.

Meaning	Masculine	Feminine
this (here)	ce sac	cette robe
these (here)	ces sacs	ces robes
that (near listener)	ce sac-ci	cette robe-ci
those (near listener)	ces sacs-ci	ces robes-ci
that (far from listener)	ce sac-là	cette robe-là
those (far from listener)	ces sacs-là	ces robes-là

Note that to express *this/that* before a masculine singular noun which starts with a vowel, "cet" is used. For example: *cet imperméable.* This rule does not hold true for feminine singular nouns beginning with a vowel. For example: *cette écharpe.*

This or That

To express *this one, that one, these* or *those* without specifically mentioning the object, use the demonstrative pronouns in the chart below.

Meaning	Masculine	Feminine	Neuter
this one (here)	celui	celle	ce (c', ç')
these (here)	ceux	celles	
that one (near listener)	celui-ci	celle-ci	ceci
those (near listener)	ceux-ci	celles-ci	
that one (far from listener)	celui-là	celle-là	cela (ça)
those (far from listener)	ceux-là	celles-là	

Use the demonstrative pronouns *ce, ceci* and *cela* when you have no specific object in mind.

In casual spoken language, *cela* is often replaced by *ça*.

Future/Conditional Irregulars

The following irregular verbs have identical changes in the stem of the verb for both the future and conditional tenses:

	Verb	Stem
to have	avoir	aur-
to have to	devoir	devr-
to send	envoyer	enverr-
to be	être	ser-
to make, do	faire	fer-
to be able to	pouvoir	pourr-
to receive	recevoir	recevr-
to know	savoir	saur-
to come	venir	viendr-
to see	voir	verr-
to want	vouloir	voudr-

Endings:

Future	Conditional
-ai	-ais
-as	-ais
-a	-ait
-ons	-ions
-ez	-iez
-ont	-aient

Irregular Participles

A few verbs have irregular **present participles:**
avoir: ayant/having, être: étant/being, savoir: sachant/knowing.
Verbs which have irregular **past participles** do not belong to the *er,*
ir, or re verb families. Some common ones are listed below.

Infinitive	Past Participle	Infinitive	Past Participle
avoir (to have)	eu	lire (to read)	lu
boire (to drink)	bu	mettre (to put [on])	mis
connaître (to be acquainted with)	connu	pouvoir (to be able to)	pu
devoir (to have to)	dû	prendre (to take)	pris
dire (to say, tell)	dit	recevoir (to receive)	reçu
écrire (to write)	écrit	savoir (to know)	su
être (to be)	été	voir (to see)	vu
ire (do make, do)	fait	vouloir (to want)	voulu

The Pronouns y and en

Y and **en** are object pronouns used to replace certain prepositional phrases to avoid sounding repetitive. They are used frequently in French. As with other object pronouns they precede the verb:

• The pronoun **y** is used to replace a preposition plus a word for a place or location. **y** can also replace **à** plus a noun representing an idea or thing, but not a person.

For example:

Allez-vous <u>à la fête</u>?   Non, je n'<u>y</u> vais pas.

Are you going <u>to the party</u>?   No, I'm not going <u>there</u>.

• Similarly, the pronoun **en** replaces the preposition **de** plus a place or almost any prepositional phrase beginning with **de**

For example:

Le train vient <u>de Paris</u>.   Mon ami <u>en</u> vient aussi.

(The train comes <u>from Paris</u>.)   (My friend comes <u>from there</u> also.)

Avez-vous besoin <u>d'eau</u>?   Non, je n'<u>en</u> ai pas besoin.

(Do you need <u>some water</u>?)   (No, I don't need <u>any</u>.)

Portions & Measurements

a dozen	**une douzaine**	inch	**un pouce**
a gallon	**un gallon**	centimeter	**un centimètre**
a handful	**une poignée**	foot	**un pied**
an ounce	**une once**	gallon	**un gallon**
a pair	**une paire**	kilogram	**un kilogramme**
a piece	**un morceau**	kilometer	**un kilomètre**
a pint	**une pinte**	liter	**un litre**
a pound	**un demi-kilo**	meter	**un mètre**
a half	**un demi**	mile	**un mile**
a quart	**un litre**	ounce	**une once**
a slice	**une tranche**	pound	**un demi-kilo**